ADVENTURES WITH GOD

Interactive Devotional for Kids & Parents

ADVENTURES WITH GOD

Interactive Devotional for Kids & Parents

by
Jennifer Wilson

Harrison House
Tulsa, Oklahoma

Adventures With God
Interactive Devotional for Kids & Parents
ISBN 1-57794-001-6
Copyright © 1998 by Jennifer Wilson
P. O. Box 580436
Tulsa, Oklahoma 74158-0463

Published by Harrison House, Inc.
P. O. Box 35035
Tulsa, Oklahoma 74153

Contents

Part 1

Part 2

A Note to Parents

Dear Parent,

The greatest privilege we have as Christian parents is to share the Word of God with our children. In today's busy world, many parents face the incredible challenge of finding such quality time. This book, *Adventures With God*, is designed to help meet that challenge. It provides daily activities for you and your preschooler to do together in 10 to 15 minute segments. Each week, you can discover a simple Scripture that leads children into an exciting adventure as they discover who God is and how very much He loves them. This book also enables parents and children to enjoy some special time together each day. The weekly lessons are simple, independent of one another, and designed to require only household supplies.

The format is that of a simple alphabet book so you can also reinforce letter recognition and sounds as you go through the year. Also, several patterns and illustrations are included for your convenience, in the back of the book.

These lessons are designed to help your child develop spiritually, mentally and emotionally. It is my prayer that you will use these activities as a guide and allow the Holy Spirit to lead you creatively, discovering your own child's interests and learning style. May you enjoy the most fulfilling task a parent can ever have — breaking open the bread of life with your precious little one.

Sincerely,
Jennifer Wilson

Supply Key

You will find the following little icons throughout the book. When you see them, you will know exactly what supplies will be needed for each week's activities.

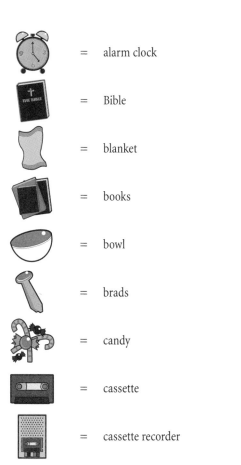

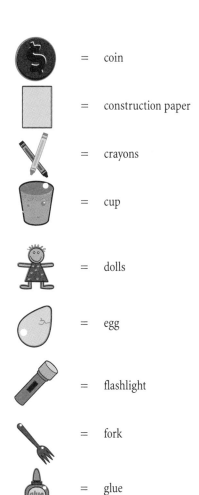

=	alarm clock	=	coin
=	Bible	=	construction paper
=	blanket	=	crayons
=	books	=	cup
=	bowl	=	dolls
=	brads	=	egg
=	candy	=	flashlight
=	cassette	=	fork
=	cassette recorder	=	glue
=	clay		

= hat

 = knife

 = markers

 = overcoat

 = paper

 = pencil

 = plate

 = poster board

 = pot

 = radio

 = scissors

 = spoon

 = stove

 = tape

 = television

 = water

 = yarn

PART 1

A

you did not receive the spirit of bondage again to fear,
but you received the Spirit of adoption
*by whom we cry out, **Abba**, Father.*

Romans 8:15

●●

Supplies

MONDAY:

Talk about family. What would it be like if your family adopted another member? We weren't born into God's family; we were adopted, but treated the same as a natural-born child. Draw a family portrait today with your child. Make sure to include Father God in your picture!

●●●●●●●●●●●●●●●●

TUESDAY:

God likes to be talked to just like parents. Have your child dictate a letter to God or make a cassette recording him praying to God. Encourage him or her to talk to God just as he does to you.

●●●●●●●●●●●●●●●●

WEDNESDAY:

Look at pictures of animals or observe them taking care of their young. (The local library or bookstore should have books on this.) Talk about how each animal takes care of its babies: the hens lead their chicks, the cats bathe their kittens, the pigs nurse their piglets, etc. Talk about how God takes care of us, too. Although we can't see Him, He makes the food that grows, He gives us sunshine for warmth and light, He gives us rain for water and people to love.

THURSDAY:

God is our heavenly Father. He lives in heaven. His Word is an invitation for us to come live with Him there after our life here is over. Using construction paper and crayons, help your child make his own invitation to give to a special friend or relative to come visit him in your home on a specific day. Allow your child to drop it in the mailbox to be sent to that person. Explain that just as the postman will deliver your child's invitation, God sent Jesus to deliver His "invitation" (the Bible) to us.

FRIDAY:

Have you ever wondered how God is three — Father, Son and Holy Spirit — in one? Today we will attempt to demonstrate how with an egg. First of all, boil an egg. Once it is cooled, let your child hold it in his hand. Ask him, "How many eggs are in your hand?" (Answer: one.) Have your child peel the egg and save the shell. Then break open the egg to reveal the yolk. Now have your child count the parts of the egg. Ask him, "How many parts does the egg have?" (Answer: three — shell, egg white and yolk.) Tell him, "This is like God: the three persons — Father, Son and Holy Spirit — in one."

B

Adventures With God

*and they came with haste and found Mary and Joseph,
and the Babe [**baby**] lying in a manger.*
Luke 2:16

● ●

Supplies

MONDAY:

Gather some pictures and/or baby clothes from your child's infancy. Show them to him and remind him that he used to be a little baby. Talk about some things that little **babies** do. Tell him that Jesus was a little baby a long time ago, too.

● ● ● ● ● ● ● ● ● ● ● ●

TUESDAY:

Read (or paraphrase) the Bible story in Luke, chapter 2. (You may want to use your child's own New Testament to show him that this special story is found in his Bible.) Discuss the fact that Jesus was a king in heaven before He was born, but when He came to earth, He had to become a little baby first, then grow up to be a man on the earth. (Philippians 2:6-8.)

WEDNESDAY AND THURSDAY:

Turn a shoe box on its side to create a miniature manger scene. The side of the box will now become the floor of the stable or barn. Fill the barn with animals and people. You may use the pattern on page 123 or draw your own. The tabs at the bottom of each picture should be folded to allow them to stand up inside the box. This will help the animals and people to stand up inside of your barn box. If you prefer, you could use plastic animals and people instead. Now cover the floor of your barn using construction paper, yarn, real hay, crayons or markers. Be creative! NOTE: If you are short on time, you may want to create a manger instead of a barn. If so, just fill the box with straw (yarn, string or small strips of paper) and place a baby doll, representing the baby Jesus, within.

FRIDAY:

Jesus came to earth to deliver the gospel to the people. Gospel means "good news." God's good news was that Jesus came to die to wash away our sin. We can have a clean heart. Today help your child clean something for someone (brother's bicycle, Dad's lunch box, the kitchen chair of another family member, etc.), then "deliver the 'good news'" about it to that person. While you both clean, talk about how Jesus "cleaned" our life from sin. What good news!

Week 2

I, even I, am He who **comforts** you.
Isaiah 51:12

Supplies

MONDAY:

Define **comforter.** Together with your child, go around the house and either point out or gather **comfortable** things: blankets, soft pillows, fluffy sweaters, soft stuffed animals, etc. Ask your child, "How do these objects bring us comfort?" and "How does the Holy Spirit bring us comfort when we need it?" (He reminds us of Scriptures that help us and give us peaceful thoughts. He also sends people to say comforting words to us.) Discuss ways that the Holy Spirit can use us to bring comfort to others (a hug, a listening ear, kind words, sharing with someone who has lost something, etc.).

TUESDAY:

Using a paper plate and crayons, divide the plate into several pie-shaped pieces. Help your child to draw a face on each section showing a different emotion. Talk about which emotions you have when you are in need of comfort from the Holy Spirit.

WEDNESDAY:

Using two dolls or two little toy men, have your child pretend that one of them is sad about something. Let him use the other one to speak words of comfort and encouragement. You may need to teach your child what to say. Explain that this second one is speaking like the Holy Spirit does to comfort people.

Supplies

THURSDAY:

Today is a story day. Have your child fill in the blanks in the following story to create his own story.

STORY: Once upon a time there was a little (boy, girl, animal or creature) who lived in a little (thing). Each day he would go out to (do something). One day while the little (boy, girl, animal or creature) was out, a terrible thing happened: (explain). The little (boy, girl, animal or creature) didn't know what to do. So he (or she) prayed and asked the Holy Spirit to help him (or her). Then came a nice (second boy, girl, animal or creature). "I have come here to help you. Here, let me (something that will remedy the "terrible thing" mentioned earlier)," said the nice (second boy, girl, animal or creature). "Hurrah!" shouted the little (first boy, girl, animal or creature). "Now everything will be fine. Thanks for letting the Holy Spirit use you to help me," said the little (first boy, girl, animal or creature). And they lived happily ever after. The end.

MORAL OF THE STORY: The Holy Spirit often uses people to bring comfort to others.

FRIDAY:

To reinforce the concept that God is three-in-one, use 3 dolls. Show your child that there are 3 dolls (people) in one family: Mommy, Daddy and child (or Mommy and 2 children, etc.). You may want to give all of the dolls a common last name to simplify this. Ask your child, "How many people or dolls are there?" (Answer: 3.) Ask, "How many families are there?" (Answer: 1.) Explain to your child that just as there are three dolls but they are one family; God is three — Father, Son and Holy Spirit — but the same God. (Note to parents: The word "God" is a collective noun as are the words "family," "group" and "team." If your child is very familiar with the concept of a team, you could use this activity with 3 of the same team hats or shirts — 3 different players, one team.)

Week 3

Christ *died* for the ungodly.
Romans 5:6

Supplies

MONDAY:

Ask your child, "What are some nice things that people have done for you?" Then have him write a thank you note to someone for being kind to him. Afterwards talk about how Jesus **died** in his place, so that he could go to heaven. Tell your child that this is the nicest thing He could have done for him and have him write Jesus a thank you note or simply have your child lift his hands to heaven and thank Him. (1 Tim. 2:8.)

TUESDAY AND WEDNESDAY:

First draw a line down the middle of a piece of poster board or large paper. Then make a collage by gluing pictures from magazines, newspaper clippings or photos on your poster board or paper. You may even want to include drawn pictures. Complete the left half of the collage on Tuesday using pictures of ungodly activities (a person in jail, a war, etc.). Use your discretion, of course, as to what photos you would want your child to see. Talk about what ungodliness means and that Christ died for us while we were being ungodly.

Then on Wednesday, complete the right half of the collage by using pictures of godly activities (family time, sharing, helping, giving, preaching, singing, etc.). Talk about what godliness means and that because Christ died for us we want to live godly lives.

THURSDAY:

Using two sticks and string, make a miniature cross. Secure the sticks with string. Talk about how painful and shameful it was for Jesus to die this way, but that He did it for us.

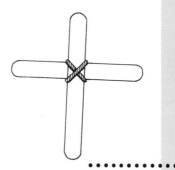

FRIDAY:

Gather some bread (or crackers) and some grape juice. Explain how the bread represents the body of Jesus broken for us, and the juice represents His blood that washes away our sins. Then take communion with your child. (1 Corinthians 11:24-25.)

Week 4 d

but the LORD *is the true God;*
*He is the living God and the **everlasting** King.*
Jeremiah 10:10

Supplies

MONDAY:

Using construction paper, crayons, scissors and a brad (or folded over paper clip), make a clock with an hour and minute hand that move. Talk about time and how **everlasting** means forever. Be sure to allow your child to turn the clock hand around several times as you talk about everlasting.

TUESDAY:

Gather old things with your child today (rocks, antiques, pictures, etc.). Ask your child, "Can we find anything that is older than God — anything that has lasted longer than God?" Of course, the answer in every case will be no.

WEDNESDAY:

Using one long strip of paper (you may need to cut several pieces and tape them together to make one long strip), cut out magazine pictures of different items and glue them onto the strip of paper. Begin on the far left of the strip with the items that would most easily tear up or wear out and end on the far right of the strip with the most enduring items. Talk about why some things are more breakable than others and how other items are more long-lasting. God isn't just long-lasting; He is everlasting.

THURSDAY:

Color a picture of God on His heavenly throne along with royal items. Cut out the royal items and paste them in the appropriate places on the picture of God.

FRIDAY:

Compare real money to play money, real jewelry to play jewelry, real food to play food, etc. Talk about the idols in the Bible. Show your child a picture of an idol or a statue. Tell him how people used to bow down and pray to these things that weren't really God. There is only one true God; He is the Lord. (The story of Elijah and the false prophets of Baal in 1 Kings 18:17-40 would be a good one to read during your family Bible reading time.)

*I have called you **friends**.*
John 15:15

• •

Supplies

MONDAY:

Ask your child, "What is a true **friend?**" Tell your child that a true friend is someone who cares about him and wants the best for him at all times. A true friend believes that he is very special. Hold your child today and tell him why you think he is so special. Then tell him that Jesus thinks he is special, too. Tell your child that Jesus even died on a cross so that when your child was born he could have a wonderful life on earth then go to heaven afterwards.

• • • • • • • • • • • • • •

TUESDAY:

Jesus is our friend. Using paper doll patterns, cut out "Jesus" and "child." Then cut out and put on the appropriate clothes for the child (boy or girl clothes) and allow your child to play paper dolls in a way that demonstrates friendship between his Jesus doll and the doll that represents himself.

WEDNESDAY:

Remind your child that a true friend will listen to the words of his friend. Show your child a Bible, preferably his own Bible. Open it to the words and explain that these are the words from his friend, Jesus. We don't hear Jesus with our ears, but He has seen to it that we have His words written down in the Bible.

THURSDAY:

True friends share with each other. Make a batch of cookies today to share with someone. Call them friendship cookies. (See page 126 for recipe.)

FRIDAY:

Invite someone special to go on a friendship picnic with you. Share a special snack and toy. Use this opportunity to tell that person why he or she is such a good friend. Take the time also to tell that person why Jesus is your good friend, too.

G

*for God so loved the world that He **gave**
His only begotten Son, that whoever believes in Him
should not perish but have everlasting life.*

John 3:16

MONDAY:

Supplies

God gave Jesus to us. He is a **giver.** Ask your child to bring his most valuable item to Bible time today. Talk about why that item is so special. Ask your child how he would feel if he was asked to give it away. Ask your child to tell you how he thinks the Father must have felt to give Jesus, His only Son.

NOTE: Set a piece of fruit outside in the sun as we will be using this for an object lesson on Thursday. Place another piece of fruit in the refrigerator and save it for Thursday, also.

TUESDAY:

Help your child make a John 3:16 bookmark out of a strip of colored paper. Let him "give it away" to someone special.

WEDNESDAY:

Make a "giving" chart. Remember to praise and reward your child for every act of giving. Remind him that he is acting like Father God each time he gives. Give a special offering in church tonight. Let your child give of his own money.

THURSDAY:

Look at the piece of fruit that you set out in the sun on Monday. What has happened to it? It has perished out in the heat. It wasn't taken care of. Have your child compare it to the piece of fruit that was being preserved in the refrigerator during that time. Share with your child that God doesn't want anyone to perish. Instead, He wants us all to be preserved blameless until the coming of the Lord. (1 Thessalonians 5:23.) Share the refrigerated fruit with your child for a snack.

FRIDAY:

Make a special reward time for your child by going to a favorite place such as a restaurant or dollar store or by doing something special together. (We call our reward time "Friday Night Fun Time.") Teach your child that you will reward him whenever he seeks to act like God, for God is a rewarder of them that diligently seek Him. (Hebrews 11:6.)

H

be holy, *for I the* LORD *your God am* holy.
Leviticus 19:2

Supplies

MONDAY:

Define **holy** as being "pure and blameless." Create an object lesson using a clear cup of clean water. Explain that this water is pure and represents a clean heart with pure motives — a holy heart. Add a handful of dirt to show your child what sin does to a clean heart. Ask your child if he has ever done something he knew was wrong and how he felt afterwards.

TUESDAY:

Make a picture puzzle with your child. Have fun practicing the verse with your child.

Be holy, for I am HOLY

WEDNESDAY:

Ask your child, "How can we be holy?" Using the same clear cup from Monday's lesson, fill it again with clean water. Remind him that this is like a person's heart that is clean and holy. Add 2 - 3 drops of food coloring to it and talk about how sin (doing wrong) pollutes the water, causing it to be unholy. Then add 1 tablespoon of bleach to the solution and stir it until the color is gone. Explain that Jesus can wash away our sin and make us

pure and holy. Remember to dispose of the bleach solution immediately after the lesson.

THURSDAY:

· · · · · · · · · · · · · ·

Practice learning how to tell the difference between right (being holy) and wrong (being unholy). Help your child look at pictures from storybooks, magazines, newspapers, etc. Talk about whether the action in the picture shows an activity that is holy or unholy. If your child is unsure, ask him if he thinks that activity would please God or not. Remember to use your discretion in choosing appropriate pictures for the age level of your child.

FRIDAY:

· · · · · · · · · · · · · ·

Let your child pick out the cases of some of his favorite videos. Ask him, "Who is the bad guy in this video?" Then ask him, "Who is the good guy?" Explain that a person's actions reveal what kind of person he really is on the inside. (Proverbs 20:11.) Holiness produces godly actions while unholiness produces sinful actions.

Week 8

I

*behold, the virgin shall conceive and bear a Son, and shall call His name **Immanuel**.*

Isaiah 7:14

• •

Supplies

MONDAY:

Immanuel means "God with us." Remind your child that God is with him even though he can't see Him. Ask your child to name things that he knows exist but that are unseen: wind, love, air, your heart, the smell of food, stars in the daytime, etc.

TUESDAY:

Today reread the story of Jesus' birth found in Luke 2:1-20. Talk about how Jesus came from heaven and was born here on earth. He was God with us. Set a place for Him at lunch today to reinforce to your child the fact that He is here. (This is also a good opportunity to teach your child how to set the table.)

WEDNESDAY:

Play a game with your child today where you pretend to be God and follow your child everywhere he goes. Then let your child pretend to be God and follow you. Emphasize that God is with us everywhere we go.

Supplies

THURSDAY:

Have your child draw a picture of himself on a piece of paper but leave a circle in the place of his face. Then cut the circle out and place a photo of your child's face under the paper in the place where the circle used to be. Next to the drawing of himself, have your child draw a picture of Jesus.

FRIDAY:

Perform a science experiment with your child today. Let your child hold a piece of ice. Explain that it is made of H_2O (2 molecules of hydrogen and 1 molecule of oxygen). Put the ice in a pot and heat it until it becomes water. Tell your child that it is still H_2O but that it looks different. Heat the water until it evaporates into steam. **Lift your child up so he can see the steam and explain that it is too hot to touch.** Tell your child that this steam is also H_2O. All three (ice, water and steam) are H_2O, but they look very different. In science, this is called a physical change.

Ask your child, "Where did the ice go?" (Answer: It became water.) Then ask your child, "Where did the water go?" (Answer: It became steam.) So, in other words, the ice became water, and the water became steam that we can't see. But even though we can't see it, it is all still with us in the air. Just as the H_2O is in the air even though we can't see it, God is with us even though we can't see Him.

J

*the **just** Lord is in the midst thereof;*
he will not do iniquity.
Zephaniah 3:5 KJV

Supplies

Monday:

Using a bathroom scale, compare the weights of some common household objects: book, rock, shoe, basketball, pot, etc. Explain to your child how the scale shows which is heavier. The scale shows the true weight of each object. That is why it is **just** or fair and so is the Lord.

Tuesday:

Take a lump of modeling clay and pull off portions of the clay in order to divide it between the two of you, making sure to divide it evenly some times and unevenly other times. Talk about what the words "fair" and "just" mean. Let your child have a turn to divide the clay fairly (justly).

Wednesday:

Practice flipping a coin. Let your child call "heads" or "tails" before the coin lands. Explain that this is sometimes used to determine who has a turn first. Ask him if he thinks it is a fair (just) way to determine this?

THURSDAY:

Compare Father God to a judge in a courtroom. If your child is unfamiliar with this concept, talk about how the judge is the one who ensures fairness to the people involved. He is an expert in the law and discerns what is right or wrong. Allow your child to put on your bathrobe and pretend to be a righteous and just judge like Father God. (2 Timothy 4:8.)

FRIDAY:

Privately read Genesis 6:5-8:22 then paraphrase for your child the story of Noah's ark. Talk about how Noah and his family were the only ones on the earth who were living a just and holy life (Refer back to Week 8 on being holy). God wanted others to be saved from the flood also, but the other people on the earth were unholy, doing bad things, because they didn't love God. No one else was saved because they wouldn't repent of their sins. God had Noah build the ark so He could save Noah and his family and all the animals and birds on the earth. Discuss how God was just, loving and fair to Noah and why He judged those people who were unholy. Let your child fingerpaint or color a beautiful rainbow. Remember to review this story and teaching each time you see a rainbow in the sky.

Week 10

K

*his merciful **kindness** is great toward us.*

Psalm 117:2

• •

Supplies

MONDAY:

Practice **kindness** today by taking something to your neighbor: a flower, baked item, picture or even their own newspaper from their driveway.

• • • • • • • • • • • • •

TUESDAY:

Help your child decorate a gift box or bag. Fill it with magazine cutouts of God's gifts to us: sun, mountains, house, car, family, food, etc.

• • • • • • • • • • • • •

WEDNESDAY:

Allow your child to call a special friend on the telephone and invite him over to your home. Before he arrives, help your child to set out several toys that he plans to share. Remind your child how he should let his guest choose the toys first. Have a special treat for your child if he is a good host. (Be sure to set specific standards for this.) Tell him about the treat before his guest arrives and remember to reward him immediately after the guest leaves. This is a very big boost for your child's self-esteem.

THURSDAY:

Make an audio tape of all the kind things your child does today. Let him talk into the tape recorder himself telling of those kind acts. Later in the evening, play his tape for someone or allow him to play his tape for someone.

FRIDAY:

Using a piece of cardboard, cut out the shape of a star. Cover it with aluminum foil and safety pin it onto your child's shirt. Let this be your child's kindness patrol badge. Supply your child with a sheet of stickers. Throughout the day, let him patrol the area looking for acts of kindness. When he finds someone doing one, allow him to give that person a sticker.

Week 11

L

God is *love*.
1 John 4:8

Supplies

MONDAY:

Help your child cut out a heart from red paper. Tell your child that a red heart is sometimes drawn in place of the word **love.** Let your child draw a picture of Jesus in the middle of the heart. Write today's verse on the heart.

TUESDAY:

Love shares. Ask your child to choose something very special of his own to share with you. Then choose something special of your own to share with your child. Exchange these items today during Bible time. Talk about how love involves both give and take. Emphasize that this is what God does with His Son, His earth and all that He has. Ask your child, "What can we share with God?" Remind your child that we are acting like God when we share.

WEDNESDAY:

You are loved. Ask your child, "Who are the people that love you?" Tape photos of these people onto a poster entitled, "I am loved." Ask your child, "How do you know that these people love you?" Talk about the actions that show love. Sing along with your child the song, "Jesus Loves Me."

THURSDAY:

Today, cut out big paper arms and tape them to the back of the "I am loved" poster your child made on Wednesday. Tell your child that the arms stand for Jesus' arms of love and that they are big enough to go around all of us.

FRIDAY:

Love does for others. Talk about what God has done for us (given us our family, died on the cross, etc.) Ask your child, "What can we do for God today?" (Answer: praise Him, show His love to someone else, prepare an offering for church, etc.) Take time to have your child select something he wants to do for God today and do it.

Week 12

M

the LORD *is* **merciful** *and gracious,*
slow to anger, and plenteous in mercy.
Psalm 103:8 KJV

Supplies

MONDAY:

Define **mercy** as "being shown kindness when you don't deserve it." Ask your child, "Has goodness or kindness ever been shown to you when you didn't deserve it?" Look for an opportunity to be merciful to each other today. For each special act of kindness, give your child a big hug.

TUESDAY:

Explain what *plenteous* means. Place a few beans or M&M's in your child's hand. Tell him that the beans in his hands are few. Then fill his hands with beans. Tell him that the beans in his hands are plenteous. Talk about how God is plenteous in mercy and never gives up on us.

WEDNESDAY:

Put a coin in your child's piggy bank and explain that you did it just because you love him, not because of anything that he or she did. This is showing mercy. Ask your child to think of something today that he can do for someone else in the same way, just because he loves that person, not because of something that person has done for him.

THURSDAY:

Help your child gather all of his stuffed animals. Review the story of Noah's ark from Week 10. Ask your child what he thinks the earth would be like if no animals had been saved from the flood. Tell your child about the mercy of God as demonstrated in this beautiful story. Let your child draw a picture of his favorite animal.

FRIDAY:

Ask your child, "Why should we show mercy?" Read the story of the man whose debt was forgiven, but chose not to forgive those who owed him. (Matthew 18:21-35.) Use several coins as you tell this story to demonstrate how much was owed. Help your child to draw a picture of the unforgiving servant, then glue toothpicks over his face to create "jail bars."

Week 13

he Himself has said, "I will **never
leave you** nor forsake you."
Hebrews 13:5

Supplies

MONDAY:

Read the poem, "My Shadow," by Robert Louis Stevenson. This poem is found on page 126.

Now go outside and look at your shadows. You may also do this inside with a lamp or flashlight. Talk about how your shadow is with you all the time and about how you can see it more at some times than at other times. Our shadow can never be separated from us (as implied in the poem). Just like the shadow, God promises to **never leave us** either.

TUESDAY:

Ask your child, "Have you ever gotten lost at the store or somewhere? Do you remember how that felt?" Assure your child that just as his mommy or daddy would never walk away and leave them at the store or place that they were lost, so God will never leave us or desert us. Take time today to teach your child his parents' full names and his phone number in case of an emergency. (We taught our two-year-old his phone number by putting it to a simple tune.)

WEDNESDAY:

Ask your child, "What are some things that you have had for a long time?" Find that special baby blanket or bedtime toy that your child has had since infancy. Compare it to the most recent toy or item your child has received. Talk about the words "a long time." God is eternal. He will be with us forever.

THURSDAY:

Play hide-and-go-seek with your child today. Relate this game to your child by telling him that although there are times when he may not think God is near, God is always as close as the nearest prayer. No matter where we go, we can never hide from God's care.

FRIDAY:

Record a message for your child on a cassette tape. Tell him that you will stand just outside of the room and that you want him to stay in the room to listen to the tape. After he listens, go back into the room with your child and talk to him about how that is similar to what Jesus did. He went to heaven, but He left the Holy Spirit and His Word here for us. Soon He will return to the earth to take us back to heaven with Him. He hasn't forsaken us.

Week 14

the Lord God **Omnipotent** reigns!
Revelation 19:6

Supplies

MONDAY:

Define **omnipotent** as "all powerful." Flex your muscles together with your child today. Let him try and lift a heavy object (like a brick or chair, depending on his size). Talk about how God is all powerful and stronger than anyone.

TUESDAY:

Show your child things around the house that need power in order to operate (electric can opener, alarm clock, toaster, etc.) Show what happens when they aren't plugged into the outlet. Explain that in that outlet lies a power source — the means necessary to operate the appliances. Just as the appliances must be plugged in to operate, we must be plugged into God to run spiritually. We must read our Bibles and pray to stay plugged in.

WEDNESDAY:

There are different demonstrations of power. Get a small piece of paper and roll it up to form a ball. Help your child experiment to see how many different ways he can get the paper to move (picking up the paper with his hands, kicking it with his feet, blowing it, using a fan, bumping it with a pencil or other object, even putting it in the sink and letting the running water move it). Emphasize to your child that God is the force behind all power.

THURSDAY:

Have a lesson in homophones. Explain to your child that *homophones* (or homonyms as many of us adults call them) are words that sound the same but have different meanings. *Reign* and *rain* are homophones. Discuss the meanings of each of the two words. Then draw a funny picture to show the two meanings such as a king floating in the air sideways as if he was a cloud with raindrops coming down below him.

FRIDAY:

Ask your child, "Who are your leaders, the people who reign in your life?" Show your child pictures of his parents, teachers, pastor and president. If pictures aren't available, point out different people in authority such as policemen and Sunday school teachers. Then help your child pray for these people in authority so you can live peaceful lives according to 1 Timothy 2:1-2.

Week 15

P

*now may the God of **patience** . . .
grant you to be like-minded toward one another.*
Romans 15:5

Supplies

MONDAY:

Play a simple game with your child (cards, ball, board game, etc.) that allows your child to practice waiting his turn. Encourage him in being patient, reminding him that God is very patient with us.

TUESDAY:

Write the word **patience** on a piece of fruit which has a removable peeling such as an orange or banana. Tell your child that patience is a fruit of the spirit. Fruit is tasty and is good for you. Patience is the same way. When we act patiently, we are acting like God. Help your child peel the piece of fruit. Talk about how it takes patience to enjoy this fruit because we must wait and patiently peel it before we can eat it.

WEDNESDAY:

Agree with your child about a specific prayer request that you can pray about today. Write it down on your calendar on today's date. Talk about how sometimes we must exercise patience between the time that we pray about something and the time that we actually see the prayer answered. Remember to write it on your calendar when the answer does manifest and talk about how your child waited patiently before he saw the answer.

THURSDAY:

Teach your child about faith and patience — the power twins. Give your child a piece of candy to put in his pocket. Tell him that this is his candy to eat after lunch. When we pray, it is like God placing the answer in our pocket. We have our answer that minute by faith. Then, we must use patience before we can partake of that answer. Thank God for an answer to prayer that is ours by faith, then use your patience until you are able to partake of that answer.

FRIDAY:

This morning, plan a very special activity with your child. This could be a Friday Night Fun Time or even just a special time of playing with your child in an activity that he selects. To learn more about patience, plan for the fun to occur in the evening or late afternoon so that your child must wait for it.

*surely I am coming **quickly**.*
Revelation 22:20

Supplies

MONDAY:

Play a game where you practice slowly and **quickly.** Call out an animal name (turtle, horse, ant, cheetah, lion, frog, etc.) and let your child go across the room as the animal might do. Talk about how some animals go slowly and others go quickly. When Jesus comes back, He is coming quickly in the twinkling of an eye. (1 Corinthians 15:52.)

TUESDAY:

Let your child boil some water with you today. Tell him to watch the water as you turn the burner on. Comment to him that the water doesn't boil right away, but that he must wait. Then just before it is about to boil, tell your child that it will begin to boil very soon (quickly). Let him watch closely as the water starts a rolling boil.

Talk about how it has been a long time since Jesus left the earth. He said He would come back to the earth quickly. Just as the water was on the stove a long while without boiling, there came a time when it was closer to boiling. Jesus has been away from the earth a long time, and now it is getting very close to the time He will return. (Caution your child about never playing with the stove or touching anything on it because it is very hot.)

WEDNESDAY:

Prepare for someone to stop by your house today. Tell your child that you must prepare for that person's coming. Allow your child to help with the house cleaning. Compare this to Jesus' return. Because Jesus is returning quickly, we must be prepared. We must make sure our house (our life) is clean and free from sin.

THURSDAY:

Use cotton balls to make clouds. Glue the clouds onto a piece of light blue paper. In between the clouds, draw Jesus descending and draw the people below rising to meet Him.

FRIDAY:

Plan a time today for cloud watching. Go outside to lie down and watch the clouds with your child. Ask your child, "What figures can you see in the clouds?" Talk about the Lord's return.

Week 17

R

*I am the **resurrection**, and the life. He who believes in Me, though he may die, he shall live.*
John 11:25

• •

Supplies

MONDAY:

Read the story of Lazarus being raised from the dead. Wrap your child in tissue paper symbolizing Lazarus' grave clothes. Let your child burst out of them as you shout, "Lazarus, come forth!" Talk about how Lazarus was **resurrected** from death to life.

• • • • • • • • • • • • • •

TUESDAY:

Use a small garden pot, some soil and a seed of some kind. Plant the seed today and explain that this is similar to a death. The seed goes into the dirt and is covered over. Later, after watering the seed and giving it sunlight, the plant will shoot forth, just like we will when the resurrection comes.

WEDNESDAY:

Using a paper plate, a small piece of construction paper, a brad and crayons, make a "4 Seasons Chart." Talk about the fact that many plants die or become dormant in the autumn and winter yet in the spring have a beautiful resurrection which yields life throughout the summer.

THURSDAY:

Talk about how water baptism is a visual picture of the death and resurrection of Jesus. Use a doll and a basin of water to teach your child that going under the water symbolizes Jesus' death and that coming out of the water symbolizes His resurrection. Tell your child that the Bible says that when He comes again, we will be raised together with Christ. (Romans 6:4,5.)

FRIDAY:

Talk about what it means to have a heart of stone or a heart of clay. Read Ezekiel 36:26. Get a rock and a piece of clay. Tell your child that a heart of stone won't allow for anyone to help, yet a heart of clay is very soft and is willing to listen to others and is open to God's help. Let your child give you the rock in exchange for the piece of clay.

Week 18

S

*I am the good **shepherd**.*
*The good **shepherd** gives His life for the sheep.*
John 10:11

• •

Supplies

MONDAY:

Jesus is the good **shepherd.** Make sheep out of cotton balls, toothpicks, and black paper. Ask your child, "Why do you think Jesus calls us His sheep?" (Answer: because the sheep follow the Shepherd.)

• • • • • • • • • • • • • • •

TUESDAY:

Play the sheep call game. First of all, the sheep hides somewhere in a room. Then Mom or Dad comes into the room and calls for the sheep who is hiding in the room. When they call, the little sheep bleats and comes to the shepherd (the mom or dad).

WEDNESDAY:

The Good Shepherd takes care of His sheep. Allow your child to hold a very special item in your home (an antique toy or something very fragile). Show your child how to hold such an object, taking great care with it. Relate this to how Jesus takes care of us because we are so special.

THURSDAY:

Read or tell the Bible story about David, the shepherd boy, killing a lion and a bear in order to save a sheep that was in his care. You may want to use stuffed animals and a slingshot or stones as you tell this story. He risked his life for the sheep. Jesus did more than that — He laid down His life for the sheep. (John 10:11.)

FRIDAY:

Let's learn about metaphors today. A *metaphor* is a figure of speech that speaks of a person or object as if it were another. For example, Jesus said, "I am the good shepherd" (John 10:11). Draw a picture of Jesus holding a shepherd's crook. To illustrate that we are His sheep, the other half of the metaphor, draw people all around Jesus standing close to Him, just as sheep would do to a shepherd.

Week 19

T

*we know that You are a **teacher** come from God.*
John 3:2

• •

Supplies

MONDAY:

Draw a teacher figure and cut out. Ask your child, "What do teachers do?" On the figure, list things teachers do (explain, show, lead, encourage, etc.) Then discuss how Jesus does all of these things as well as school or Sunday school teachers.

TUESDAY:

Jesus is our **teacher.** His Spirit teaches us when we read the Bible and pray. Recognize your favorite teacher today by coloring and cutting out the "Best Teacher Award." (See page 127.) Have fun presenting it to your favorite teacher the next time you see him or her. Remember to thank Jesus for being your teacher, also.

WEDNESDAY:

The Bible is the best school book ever. Remind your child that we love the Bible because it is God's Word to us. Let your child select a Bible story today. Ask him, "What lesson did this story teach us?"

THURSDAY:

Our parents are very important teachers. Help your child to make a special note for you today and write (or dictate to you) some of the very special things he learns from you. (You may also want to tell your child some of the lessons you have learned from him.)

FRIDAY:

Using sidewalk chalk, allow your child to draw on the driveway or sidewalk. Ask him to draw his class at church and his teachers.

Week 20

U

the LORD by wisdom founded the earth;
*By **understanding** He established the heavens.*

Proverbs 3:19

* *

Supplies

MONDAY:

Show your child the family tool box. Describe or show the purpose of several different tools. Tell your child that wisdom and **understanding** are tools that were used by God to build the earth and the heavens.

· · · · · · · · · · · · · ·

TUESDAY:

What is **understanding?** To teach this, use an example of simple subtraction. Tell your child you will teach him subtraction today. Set out four raisins on a table. Allow him to take one away and eat it. Tell him that he has just subtracted one raisin from the four raisins. Now he has three left. Ask him to subtract another raisin. When he takes another one away, tell him that he has just subtracted one raisin from the three remaining raisins. Now he has two left.

Praise him for understanding subtraction. He probably won't be able to define the word, or explain the concept, but you know that he now understands the new word. God is the source of all understanding.

WEDNESDAY:

Being confused is the opposite of understanding. Tell your child that you are going to give him instructions on how to do something in two different ways. Ask him to tell you which one he understands more clearly. First, ask him to get a shirt from his drawer. Secondly, ask him to get his *green* shirt from the *bottom* drawer in his bedroom. Now, ask him to tell you which instruction he understood more clearly. Explain that when we read God's Word, we get a clear picture of God's plan for the whole world.

THURSDAY:

Use a globe or basketball to teach your child about the shape of the earth. At night, go outside and look at the stars and the moon. Explain that God created the earth by His wisdom. Point out that the heavens are above the earth and that by His understanding He established the heavens.

FRIDAY:

Pull a weed from your yard or garden. Show your child a taproot (dandelion roots, crabgrass roots, or even carrots are good examples). Tell your child that the root is what establishes the plant. It keeps it from blowing away. God's understanding is like a taproot. When we read it and apply it to our lives, it helps to establish us, too.

Week 21

*I am the **vine**, you are the branches.*
He who abides in Me, and I in him, bears much fruit;
for without Me you can do nothing.

John 15:5

• •

Supplies

MONDAY:

Find a vine in your yard or neighborhood. Point out the two metaphors in this verse: Jesus is the **vine,** and we are the branches. Point out the vine to your child, comparing it to Jesus — the source of our life. Then point out the branches, comparing them to believers — ones who come from the vine.

NOTE: Pull one branch off of the vine and keep it for Friday.

TUESDAY:

Using green construction paper, make a vine. Don't add branches or leaves yet. Label this vine "Jesus."

WEDNESDAY:

Add some green branches to your "Jesus vine." Label these branches using your child's name, the names of other members of your family or other Christians that you both know.

Supplies

THURSDAY:

Today create some beautiful fruit for the branches. Label them "love," "joy," "peace," "patience," "gentleness," "goodness," "kindness," "faithfulness" and "self control." Remind your child that the vine helps those branches to bear good fruit, which is their job.

FRIDAY:

Look at the branch that was broken off of the vine on Monday. Ask your child, "Why do you think it has withered?" Use this to show your child the importance of knowing Jesus. Without Him, we, too, will wither spiritually.

Week 22

W

*fear not, for I am **with you**.*
Isaiah 41:10

• •

Supplies

MONDAY:

Show your child some photographs from family vacations. Remind him that God was **with him** in each place that he went.

• • • • • • • • • • • • •

TUESDAY:

Using two dolls (or action figures), show your child that God is with us wherever we go. Have your child choose one doll to be like God. Then have the one doll that is representing God walk beside the other doll wherever it goes.

• • • • • • • • • • • • •

WEDNESDAY:

Hold your child's hand as you enter a dark room or closet. Talk about how he doesn't have to fear because Mommy or Daddy is with him. Tell him that even when a parent isn't near, God is always **with him.**

THURSDAY:

Soak an old rag in a solution of 1 part water and 1 part rubbing alcohol. Read the Bible story of Shadrach, Meshach and Abednego in the fiery furnace. (Daniel 3:1-30.) Be prepared to tell the story to your child in your own words.

Emphasize to your child that these boys weren't afraid of King Nebuchadnezzar or the fiery furnace because they knew that God was with them. During the story, pull the soaked rag out of the solution using an opened wire hanger or long stick. Then light the rag with a match. Watch as it flames but never burns the cloth. Talk about how God was with these three boys in the fire, protecting them. (Note to parents: this activity should be done outside on the driveway or on concrete where there are no flammable objects nearby. Be sure to have the child stand back away from the flame. Have a bucket of water nearby to extinguish the flame if necessary. Pour out the water and alcohol mixture immediately after the activity.)

FRIDAY:

Allow your child to boil an egg. While it is boiling, tell your child about Noah. Tell him how Noah preached while he was building the ark, but no one believed him. (Genesis 6:11-9:17.) He had a good opportunity to be afraid of what the people thought about him, but he knew that God was with him. Once the egg is boiled, peel it, slice it in half, scoop out the yolk and float the two little egg-arks in a shallow basin of water as you review this week's verse.

X

*o LORD our Lord, how **excellent** is
Your name in all the earth.*
Psalm 8:1

• •

Supplies

MONDAY:

Practice handwriting today using the letter "X." Show your child how the "X" can be turned to look like Jesus' cross. Gather 2 sticks and form the letter "X" and then form a cross.

• • • • • • • • • • • •

TUESDAY:

What does the word **excellent** mean? It can mean very good, or it can be a title of dignity. Tell your child that some people, who are kings and queens, are even called "your excellency" to show respect. Help your child to make his own name plate (a sign of dignity) by folding a piece of paper with his name written on it.

• • • • • • • • • • • •

WEDNESDAY:

Jesus has an excellent name. Practice writing the word "Jesus." As you go through the day, be on the lookout for the letters in His name on license plates, billboards, magazines, etc.

THURSDAY:

Talk to your child about his name. Does it have a special meaning? Was he or she named after a particular person? If so, why? Tell your child why you like his name. Tell your child that *Jesus* is another way of saying Joshua and means "Jehovah is salvation or Savior" and that *Christ* means the "Anointed One." This name was chosen by Father God Himself.

The Bible tells us that someday everyone who hears that name will bow and confess that He is Lord. (Philippians 2:10,11.) Let your child form his own name and the name of Jesus out of modeling clay or write the names, using his fingers, in a pan filled with whipped cream or shaving cream.

FRIDAY:

Explain to your child that we are to pray to the Father in the name of Jesus. (John 15:16.) Show your child the mail that comes to your house. Help him to point out your family's name on the envelopes. Explain that we get this mail because of our name. Other people don't get to receive our letters because they don't have our name. If we want the blessings of God, we must use Jesus' name because each blessing is first sent to Him then forwarded on to us.

Week 24

*for all the promises of God in Him are **Yes**,
and in Him Amen.*

2 Corinthians 1:20

● ●

Supplies

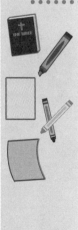

MONDAY:

Using noisemakers, practice making joyful noises! Drums can be made from old oatmeal cartons, shakers from beans in a "sippy cup", etc. After you and your child recite the verse for the week, allow your child to yell, **"Yes!"** and "Amen!" which means, "yes" and "so be it".

NOTE: Put noisemakers aside for use next week.

● ● ● ● ● ● ● ● ● ● ● ● ● ●

TUESDAY:

Tell your child that God answers **"yes"** and "amen" to all of the promises in the Bible. Make a Bible by inserting one piece of folded white paper inside one piece of folded black paper and stapling them together along the fold. Now, open up the cover of your Bible and help your child write, "Yes!" and "Amen!" on the first page of the white paper.

NOTE: Put the Bible in a special place so that your child can easily get to it for the rest of the activities in the week.

WEDNESDAY:

On the second and third page of the folded white paper in the Bible that your child made yesterday, help your child write or draw pictures to represent "long life" (Psalm 91:16), "health" (3 John 2), "needs met" (Philippians 4:19), "joy" (John 15:11), "abundant life on earth" (John 10:10) and "everlasting life" (John 3:16). Tell them that these are some of the promises found in the Bible.

THURSDAY:

Turn to page 4, the last white page of your homemade Bible, and write in or draw pictures that represent some more promises and scriptural references: "loved one's salvation" (Acts 16:31), "desires of your heart" (Psalm 37:4), "favor with others" (Psalm 5:12).

FRIDAY:

Make a prayer journal with your child by inserting two folded pieces of white paper into one folded piece of colored paper and stapling them together along the fold. Using crayons, write "journal" on the front cover and let your child decorate it. Then turn to the first page and draw two columns. At the top of the first column write, "prayer request and date." (Be sure to include the Bible promise that corresponds to the request. Your child may want to refer back to the Bible he made.) At the top of the second column write, "praise report and date." Continue to add to your prayer journal as needs arise. Younger children can cut out and paste pictures in the journal to represent their request.

Week 25

Z

*for He put on righteousness as a breastplate,
and a helmet of salvation on His head . . .
and was clad with **zeal** as a cloak.*

Isaiah 59:17

● ●

Supplies

MONDAY:

Explain to your child that **zeal** is excitement and enthusiasm about something. Take turns naming words that rhyme with zeal (seal, peel, reel, etc.)

TUESDAY:

Allow your child to play dress-up today. Use an oversized shirt for the breastplate of righteousness, a hat for the helmet of salvation and a coat for the zeal of the Lord.

WEDNESDAY:

Act out opposites today. Call out several activities that your child can act out zealously and also lethargically (swimming in a big pool, climbing a tall mountain, eating dinner, etc.)

THURSDAY:

Look in books, magazines or on the television for demonstrations of zealousness (check the sports page or ESPN for several examples). Discuss things for which God shows zealousness: justice, helping His children, punishing the wicked, blessing the righteous, etc.

FRIDAY:

Create a cheer for God. Using the noisemakers that you made last week, show your own zealousness for God's goodness to you by making up and performing a cheer together.

PART 2

Adventures With God

A how God **anointed** Jesus of Nazareth with the Holy Spirit and with power, who went about doing good and healing all who were oppressed by the devil, for God was with Him.

Acts 10:38

• •

Supplies

MONDAY:

The **anointing** is "God's ability working in you." Ask your child to reach into a closet to get a shirt that he can't reach, while you stand next to him. After several attempts, explain to him that you asked him to get the shirt knowing he couldn't reach it. Now lift him up to get the shirt. Ask him, "Who got the shirt down?" (Answer: I did, but with help from you.) Tell your child that we do many things on earth, but that it is God's help — His anointing within us — that causes them to get done.

• • • • • • • • • • • • • •

TUESDAY:

The anointing breaks the yoke. Talk about how we sometimes face difficult burdens in our lives. Then lay a heavy quilt over your child's shoulders behind his neck. Compare this to an animal's yoke so that your child can understand that a yoke is heavy and keeps him attached to another animal or cart.

Ask your child, "Would you get tired if you had that heavy quilt over your shoulders all day?" (Answer: yes.) When people have burdens, it sometimes feels like a heavy yoke. Read Isaiah 10:27 together with your child and show him that the Bible says that it is the anointing that breaks the yoke.

WEDNESDAY:

We can keep the anointing flowing in our lives by doing good works. (1 Peter. 3:8,9.) Use an empty paper towel roll and bend it over. Ask your child to try to push a sock through it from the top to the bottom. Tell your child that we hinder the power of God — the anointing — operating in our lives if we aren't doing good works. But when we maintain good works (straighten out the tube), the anointing can be seen in our lives much more easily. Have your child push the sock through the tube.

THURSDAY:

We are the Body of Christ. (Romans 12:5.) Make a body today out of your child's clothes (long-sleeved shirt, jeans, shoes and gloves) stuffed with other clothes or towels. Use a small basketball or soccer ball for the head. On the ball, tape a paper plate that has a picture of Jesus' face drawn on it. Use this as a tool to show your child how He is the head, and we are His body. And if we are His Body, we should have His anointing operating in us and through us at all times.

FRIDAY:

Add to your prayer journal. Pray today for your child's teachers and leaders. Pray that they would flow in the anointing of God to lead your child and the others whom they lead. (Ephesians 6:19.) Remember to write the date of the request and the Scripture reference.

Week 27

B

*as for God . . . he is a **buckler** [shield and protector]
to all those that trust in him.*
Psalm 18:30 KJV

Supplies

MONDAY:

Use a piece of poster board to make a large shield for your child to hold. (See page 128.) Help him to write, "God," on the front of the shield. Let him play with the shield as you talk about the protection that a shield gives.

TUESDAY:

Ask your child, "Who are some people who act as our **'bucklers'** or 'protectors' on earth?" Look for policemen, firemen and lifeguards throughout the day. You may even want to drive by the police station or fire station so that your child can meet some of these people.

WEDNESDAY:

Talk about "all those that trust Him" today. To show your child about trust, have him stand up with his back toward you. Tell him to fall backwards into your arms without looking. Assure him that you will catch him. After you catch your child, praise him for his trust in you. Compare this to our trust in God.

THURSDAY:

Let your child get his Bible so you can read to him Psalm 91:4. First find the word "buckler" in the verse. Tell him what it means when the Bible says that the truth shall be our "buckler."

Then draw and color a picture of a feather or pull a feather from your feather duster and talk about what he thinks, "He will cover you with His feathers," means. Ask your child, "Have you ever seen how a mother bird protects her young?" If possible, show Your child a picture of this while you explain. Then tell your child that God takes care of us in a similar way.

FRIDAY:

Get out your child's life jacket. Let him put it on. Discuss how the life jacket protects him when he is in a boat or in the water. Gather other items that are designed for protection: ear muffs, gloves, hard hat, goggles and sun screen lotion. Talk about how they also protect him. These things remind us of God because He is the Great Protector, our Buckler!

C

*in the beginning God **created** the heavens and the earth.*
Genesis 1:1

. . . .

Supplies

MONDAY:

Look in the mirror with your child. If possible, have him stand with his back to a full-length mirror then have him hold a hand-held mirror in front of his face in such a way that he can see the image of himself in the full-length mirror. Teach him to say, "God **created** me like Him!"

TUESDAY:

Create your own modeling clay today. Make the "Peanut Butter Play Clay" then have your child form it into the figures of special people that God has created. Remember, your child can eat his sculptures when he is finished!

Recipe for Peanut Butter Play Clay
  1 cup peanut butter
  $^1/_2$ cup honey
  1 cup powdered milk
Combine all ingedients. Roll into desired shapes and eat.

WEDNESDAY:

God created the animals. Visit the zoo, pet store or even a neighbor's back yard to have a hands-on experience with an animal. Talk about how God created all the animals. Ask your child, "What is your favorite animal?" and "Why?"

THURSDAY:

God created the earth. Go on a creation walk and take a bag to collect samples of items that God has created.

FRIDAY:

God created the heavens. Tonight, look at the stars and moon with your child. Talk about how God created all the heavens.

D

*I am the **door**. If anyone enters by Me, he will be saved.*
John 10:9

• •

Supplies

MONDAY:

Using a piece of dark blue paper, red paper and bright yellow paper, make a Jesus **door.** (See page 129.)

• • • • • • • • • • • • •

TUESDAY:

Find three cups that are the same. Tell your child that one cup represents Jesus, one represents an idol and one represents good works. Place a little surprise under one of them (a new eraser, piece of candy, coin, etc.). Tell your child that the prize is only under the one that represents Jesus. Mix the cups around. Let your child choose the cup which he thinks contains the prize. Let him continue to try until he finds the prize. Jesus is the only door to the blessings of God.

• • • • • • • • • • • • •

WEDNESDAY:

Help your child to write, "Jesus," on a rectangular piece of poster board then tape it on the door. Place your child's favorite toy behind the door that he has labeled "Jesus." Emphasize again that Jesus is the door.

THURSDAY:

Find a large cardboard box. Turn it upside down, then let your child use markers to draw the heavens at the top of the box and the earth at the bottom of the box. When he is completed, have him draw little ladders from the earth to the heavens that aren't quite tall enough to reach. Explain to him that these ladders represent man's attempts to reach God on his own: good works, false religions, idol worship, wishing, etc.

After discussing these useless attempts, tell your child that Father God sent His own ladder — His Son, Jesus. Have your child draw a ladder from heaven down to the bottom of the box. This ladder was the law found in the Old Testament. Jesus was sent to climb this ladder so that no other man could climb it. He fulfilled the law. (Matthew 5:17.) Now, we are to accept Him. This is God's grace. (Ephesians 2:8.)

FRIDAY:

Play "Jesus Says" like "Simon Says." Call out simple directions, but your child should only do the ones that you say, "Jesus says," beforehand.

E

the LORD *is* **exalted***, for He dwells on high.*

Isaiah 33:5

• •

Supplies

MONDAY:

First of all, make a paper airplane with your child. Then color and cut out a picture of Jesus' upper body and insert it into the airplane. Tell your child that **exalted** means "lifted up" and have your child fly the plane as he practices this week's verse.

• • • • • • • • • • • • •

TUESDAY:

Have your child lay down on his back with his tummy showing. Tell your child the story on page 130 as he watches his tummy go up and down. He should make his tummy go up when he hears the word "up" and down when he hears the word "down." Talk about how this story is similar to the story of Jesus.

• • • • • • • • • • • • •

WEDNESDAY:

Finger paint a picture of heaven. Tell your child about the golden streets (Revelation 21:21), the colored walls (Revelation 21:18-20), the great river coming from God's throne (Revelation 22:1) and the tree of life (Revelation 22:2).

THURSDAY:

Using modeling clay, make a model of the throne of God. Allow your child to place it in a high place because God is exalted. You may want to use the "Peanut Butter Play Clay" recipe already given on page 70.

FRIDAY:

We are seated with Christ in heavenly places. (Ephesians 2:6.) Out of modeling clay, have your child form another throne with a small clay figure of himself seated in it. Place this throne beside the one from yesterday and read aloud the Scripture from Ephesians 2:6.

F

Adventures With God

*God is **faithful**, by whom you were called into the fellowship of His Son, Jesus Christ our Lord.*
1 Corinthians 1:9

● ●

Supplies

MONDAY:

Let Mom or Dad pretend to be Father God. Have your child hold a Bible and walk around. Follow him, explaining that God is **faithful.** He stands behind His Word no matter what.

○ ○ ○ ○ ○ ○ ● ● ● ● ● ● ●

TUESDAY:

Use a toy telephone or unplugged real one to emphasize to your child that God has called us. Talk about how we know He has called us. It isn't because we received a phone call from God, but because He tells us through His Word, the Bible.

● ● ● ● ● ● ● ● ● ● ● ●

WEDNESDAY:

God is faithful, and we are to be faithful, too. Make a game of picking up the pieces of a puzzle in the midst of distractions (door opening, alarm clock going off, parent going in and out of the room, etc.). Explain that we are to be faithful to whatever task God asks us to do, even though there may be many distractions around us.

THURSDAY:

Go for a walk with your child today. Observe and talk about what things he can count on to be the same day after day. When you get home, have your child draw a picture of one of the things that you talked about while on your walk.

FRIDAY:

Allow your child to watch the weather on television with you or listen to the weather on the radio. Let your child hold a toy microphone (a hairbrush will do). Let him pretend to be a forecaster, talking about the soon return of Jesus.

Tell your child that we can look at the signs of the times to know that the season for Jesus' return is very soon. Jesus is faithful to His Word and will return. We can count on it, just as we can count on our four natural seasons: winter, spring, summer and autumn.

Week 32

good *and upright is the* Lord.
Psalm 25:8

• •

Supplies

Monday:

Make a sign out of green paper that says, "God," and another sign, using red paper, that says, "Devil." Talk about how God is **good,** and the devil is evil. (John 10:10.) Have your child hold up the appropriate sign when you call out different words: "family" (God), "sickness" (Devil), "friends" (God), "crime and hate" (Devil), etc.

• • • • • • • • • • • • •

Tuesday:

Pretend to be a detective today with your child. Let him wear an overcoat and hat and hold a magnifying glass if you have one. Look in the newspaper for both positive and negative articles. Ask your child "Who was responsible for this? — God or the devil?"
REMEMBER: God is good, and the devil is evil.

• • • • • • • • • • • • •

Wednesday:

Ask your child, "What is 'good' behavior?" Let him act out several behaviors that you would generally acknowledge as good (saying "please" and "thank you," raising your hand before talking, sharing with others, etc.)

THURSDAY:

Teach your child the song, "God Is So Good." (Words listed below.) Sing this with your child and talk about the many good things that God does for us. You may create new verses with your child's suggestions ("He answers prayer," "He heals the sick," "He meets my needs," etc.)

God Is So Good
God is so good. God is so good.
God is so good. He's so good to me.

FRIDAY:

Using your child's prayer journal from week 25, have your child illustrate in the "request" column several good behaviors that he plans to implement today. Have him pray and ask God to help him accomplish them.

Week 33

H

Adventures With God

*I am the Lord who **heals** you.*
Exodus 15:26

● ●

Supplies

MONDAY:

Look at a picture of a zebra. Talk about how Jesus was beaten and got thirty-nine stripes on His back that bled. Each stripe stands for a category of disease. It is because He received these stripes that we can be **healed**. (Isaiah 53:4-6.)

TUESDAY:

Using paper strips, write the name of a sickness or disease on each one. As your child repeats the verse, have him tear up a strip of paper, thus representing the elimination of that sickness through faith in God.

WEDNESDAY:

On a piece of paper, trace your child's hands. Read the Scripture, Mark 16:18b: "They shall lay hands on the sick and they shall recover." Tell your child that the Lord is our healer and that He uses His Body (believers) to be a channel of His healing power.

THURSDAY:

Wrap up a gift box or gift bag with a sign labeled "health" inside. Let your child open it and see that God has given health to him as a gift.

FRIDAY:

Healing is the children's bread. (Matthew 15:22-28.) Give your child a piece of a loaf of bread. Ask him to tell you all of the different ways that he likes to eat this kind of bread. Talk about how often people eat bread. Healing is compared to bread and is another metaphor. It is a staple of life — a necessity. Then, you may want to allow him to fix his favorite sandwich.

Week 34

*[Jesus] is the image of the **invisible** God,*
the firstborn over all creation.
Colossians 1:15

• •

MONDAY:

Go outside and feel the wind (or stand in front of a fan or heater). Talk about how you can't see the wind, but it is real. Make a paper pin wheel (See page 131.) and write, "**Invisible** God," on it. Take turns saying this week's verse and blowing the pinwheel.

TUESDAY:

Go on a listening walk with your child. Talk about all of the things that you know are close by because you can hear them, not see them.

WEDNESDAY:

Ask your child to tell you how he thinks God looks. Have your child paint a picture of God using finger paints.

THURSDAY:

Do a sequencing activity with your child. Ask him, "What came first?" Give him several different pairs: train engine then caboose, money then ice cream cone, baby picture then recent picture, etc. Talk about the fact that Jesus is the firstborn of all creation.

FRIDAY:

Use a piece of newsprint (or plain thin paper) and crayons. Have your child do some "texture rubbings" by placing the paper over an object and rubbing the crayon across the paper, thus producing the image on the paper. Some examples are a brick, the bottom of a tennis shoe, a hardwood floor, a tile and a window screen. Talk about how the images are similar and different from the original object. Jesus is the image of God the Father.

*Then I will go to the altar of God, to God my exceeding **joy**;
and on the harp I will praise You.*

Psalm 43:4

Supplies

MONDAY:

Take time today to tickle your child. Roll up tiny strips of paper that have "ha, ha, ha" and "hee, hee, hee" written on them. Put them in an empty medicine or vitamin bottle. Tell your child that "a merry heart doeth good like a medicine" (Proverbs 17:22). Then open the bottle every day this week and take out a dose of joy by pulling out a strip of paper and tickling each other to keep your joy level full.

TUESDAY:

Let your child get out all of his musical instruments today, either bought or homemade. Let your child make a **joyful** noise unto the Lord as he sings his favorite song to the Lord.

WEDNESDAY:

What makes you happy? Each one of you draw one thing that the other person does that makes you happy. Then draw one thing that God does for you that makes you happy, too.

THURSDAY:

Make an instrument today. Take the lid off of an old shoe box and place 4 or 5 rubber bands around the box so that part of the rubber band is stretched across the open part of the box, or cut out the shape of a guitar from the lid of the box and place the rubber bands around the middle. (See page 132.) Then have your child play his instrument and sing a praise song to Jesus.

FRIDAY:

As the first line of an old song goes, "Joy is the flag flown high from the castle of my heart." Using construction paper, a drinking straw and tape, make a flag. Let your child wave his flag and sing a joyful song for Jesus.

Week 36

K

and He [Jesus] has on His robe and on His thigh a name written: **KING OF KINGS**, *AND LORD OF LORDS.*

Revelation 19:16

• •

Supplies

MONDAY:

Jesus is King of all the kings of the world. Make a crown out of yellow construction paper or poster board. Then decorate the crown (use markers, foil, costume jewelry, yarn, buttons, etc.) and allow your child to be king for the day.

NOTE: Save the crown for an activity later in the week and during weeks 42, 44 and 45.

• • • • • • • • • • • • • • • •

TUESDAY:

Together, take the tune of your child's favorite song or commercial jingle and change the words. Make the song about Jesus being the **King of kings.** For example: "Old MacDonald Had a Farm" can be changed to "Jesus is the Son of God, Ha-lay-lu-jah. He's the King of everything, Ha-lay-lu-jah," etc. You may want to write the words down as you and your child compose it so that you both will be able to perform your song for Daddy when he gets home from work!

WEDNESDAY:

Using markers and a long piece of paper, have your child make a banner to wear on his thigh that reads, "King of Kings and Lord of Lords." Tuck the top of the banner in his waistband and let the rest hang down vertically over his thigh.

THURSDAY:

Show your child a globe or map. Have him place the crown on it. Talk about how Jesus is King over all of the earth.

FRIDAY:

At Jesus' second coming, He will return riding a white horse. (Revelation 19:11.) Let your child practice riding a stick-horse today. If your child doesn't have one, trace and cut out the two sides of a horse's head on paper. (See page 133.) Attach them to either side of the straw part of a broom and tie a yarn to the stick part of the broom so that he can use them for reins.

L

*God is **light** and in Him is no darkness at all.*

1 John 1:5

• •

MONDAY:

Have some flashlight fun with your child tonight. Allow him to hold a flashlight and walk around the house or yard discovering his surroundings with the flashlight. Remember to rehearse this week's verse with your child while you are on your walk. Point out that wherever there is light, the darkness goes away.

TUESDAY:

Go on a night walk around the neighborhood or house. Notice all the things that give off light of some kind: street lights, car lights, interior house lights, lightening bugs, moon, etc. Point out that just as bugs are always drawn to a light, people will be drawn to God's **light** in us. Practice the verse on your walk tonight.

WEDNESDAY:

With binoculars or a telescope, look at the stars and moon with your child tonight. (If you don't have these, you may create your own telescope using an empty paper towel roll.) Talk about the natural lights that God placed in the heavens to keep the evenings from being totally dark.

NOTE: You will use your telescope again during week 47.

THURSDAY:

Create a symmetrical drawing today to illustrate light and dark colors. (See page 134.) Have your child draw a simple drawing with a soft lead pencil only on one half of the piece of paper, pressing down very hard. Fold the paper over and press it together, thus transferring the lines of his drawing to the other side of the paper. Have your child use dark shades of crayons to color the side with the dark lines and use light shades of crayons to color the side with the light lines. (This is a good activity to reiterate the truth that Jesus is the exact expression of God, and we are made in God's image.)

FRIDAY:

Heaven will be a bright place. (Revelation 22:5.) Turn on all the lights in the house as you talk about heaven's light.

Week 38

Adventures With God

M

this man doeth many **miracles**.

John 11:47 *KJV*

● ●

MONDAY:

Read the story of Jesus turning water into wine in John 2:1-11. Privately, drop a few drops of food coloring into a large opaque pitcher. Tell the story to your child. At the point where Jesus asks for empty water pots, let your child pick up the "empty" pitcher.

At the point where the servants fill the water pots, let him fill it with water. Then allow him to pour the "wine" (colored water) into a glass at the point in the story that the servants present the wine. Explain to your child that you performed a trick, not a miracle, to illustrate to him this story. Jesus didn't do tricks, but He did do **miracles.**

● ● ● ● ● ● ● ● ● ● ● ● ● ●

TUESDAY:

Read the story of blind Bartimaeus in Mark 10:46-52. Place a blindfold or scarf over your child's eyes and lead him around the house. Let him describe how it feels to be blind. Remove the blindfold and encourage him to tell you how he thinks Bartimaeus felt to receive his sight.

● ● ● ● ● ● ● ● ● ● ● ● ● ●

WEDNESDAY:

With supervision, allow your child to sew a few stitches in a piece of scrap material with a large plastic needle and embroidery thread. Then read Psalm 139:13 from an *Amplified Bible*. Let your child compare his sewing to God weaving us in our mother's womb miraculously. Explain that we are a miracle.

THURSDAY:

Prepare the following at least 2 hours in advance. Using four small boxes of blue gelatin, follow the package directions using only half of the water required. Place two sheets of clear plastic wrap in a clear glass 9 x 12 baking dish. Make sure the two sheets of plastic wrap overlap in the middle of the pan. (See page 135.) Fill each side with the gelatin mixture holding up the center pieces of plastic wrap to keep the gelatin separated into two sides of the dish. Refrigerate until firm.

Now read the story of Moses and the parting of the Red Sea. As you read, slowly pull the center pieces of plastic wrap up and apart from each other, thus making two "walls" of blue gelatin. This will resemble the parting of the Red Sea where the children of Israel walked right down the middle. Remind your child that God hasn't changed and that He is the same in the Old Testament as in the New Testament and still today.

FRIDAY:

Read the story of Jesus multiplying the loaves and the fishes in Mark 6:33-43. To illustrate the story, bring your child's lunch box, a deep basket containing 20-30 saltine crackers, and 5 other crackers. Do not let your child see that you have these crackers already in the basket. Put the 5 crackers in the lunch box as you tell your child about the little boy's lunch of 5 loaves and 2 fish.

Have your child empty his 5 crackers into the basket as you tell him that the boy brought his lunch to Jesus. Make sure to hold the large basket high enough so that your child cannot see inside it when he is emptying his crackers into it. As you tell him that Jesus multiplied the loaves and fishes to feed everyone, empty the entire basket of crackers onto the table. Explain to your child that you had placed extra crackers in your basket ahead of time to illustrate to him this story but that Jesus really did multiply the loaves and the fishes.

Week 39

N

*but now in Christ Jesus you who once were
far off have been made **near** by the blood of Christ.*

Ephesians 2:13

• •

Supplies

MONDAY:

Talk about opposites today. Write the word "opposites" on a paper bag. Now go around the house and collect opposites: things that are smooth and rough, pointed and round, clean and dirty, moist and dry, heavy and light, thick and thin, etc. Then demonstrate the opposite of far and near. Emphasize that because of Jesus we can always be **near** to God.

• • • • • • • • • • • • • •

TUESDAY:

Help your child make a paper chain out of red construction paper. Tape it across the doorway. On the paper, write "the blood of Christ." Ask your child to break through the chain to enter the room "through the blood of Christ" as he practices this week's verse.

WEDNESDAY:

Tell your child that the blood of Christ can be compared to a car. It is what takes you somewhere. Just as your car takes you to church or to the store, the blood of Christ is what takes you to Father God. During the next two days, make a Jesus car, using a large cardboard box. Fold in the top of the cardboard box and cut a large square out of the bottom. (See page 136.) Allow your child to paint the four outer sides with red paint (or marker) and let it dry.

THURSDAY:

To complete the Jesus car, attach four paper plate wheels using butterfly clasps (brads). Then attach two old belts or ties to the front and back of the box so that they will rest on your child's shoulders like suspenders when he steps into the box. You may wish to attach yellow paper bowls for headlights and taillights or simply paint them on. Practice "near" and "far" with the Jesus car.

FRIDAY:

Look on a map or globe. Show your child where you live. What places are near your home? What places are far from your home? Before Jesus, Father God was very far away from us, but the blood of Christ brought us near Him. Invite your child to pray to the Father at this point. Encourage him to talk to God just as he talks to you.

Week 40

O

*one God and Father of all, who is above all,
and through all, and in you all.*

Ephesians 4:6

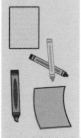

Supplies

MONDAY:

Place several pieces of white paper onto one piece of colored paper then fold in half to form a book. Staple down the middle in order to secure the pages. On the cover, write: "My Counting Book, by (your child's name)." On the first page, help your child write, "1 God," and draw a picture of the **One** Who is the Father of us all. On the second page, write, "2 people," and draw a picture of Adam and Eve. On page three, write, "3 in 1," and draw the Father, Son and Holy Spirit.

TUESDAY:

Make a mobile using a wire hanger. With yarn, attach a drawing of Father God to the center of the hanger. From the two side wires of the hanger that slant up towards the center, attach cut-out magazine pictures of things that represent heaven (river, fruit trees, bright sunlight, large banquet table filled with food, etc.)

Then, in the center of the bottom wire, attach a picture of your child. On either side of his picture, continue to use yarn to attach magazine cut-outs of familiar places on earth (the playground, family dinner table, tree house, etc.) Using longer pieces of yarn, attach pictures of things below the surface of the earth (ocean water, layers of rock, a tunnel or subway, or even construction workers digging a building's foundation). (See page 137.)

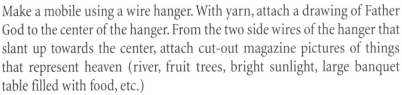

WEDNESDAY:

Teach your child the meaning of the word, "through." Together, make a tunnel through the kitchen chairs by draping a large blanket over them. Crawl through the tunnel with your child then explain to him that God is "through all."

• • • • • • • • • • • • • •

THURSDAY:

Teach your child the meaning of the word, "in." Explore with your child some special places in your home that they can go "in" (closets, attic, basement, large cabinet, storage building, etc.) Tell your child that God is "in all."

• • • • • • • • • • • • • •

FRIDAY:

Create an obstacle course using chairs, cushions, small tables, etc. to evaluate your child's knowledge of "above," "through" and "in." Tell your child to sit in the chair, crawl under the small table, stand above the cushion, etc. Remember to keep it safe as you create. When you finish, remind your child that God the Father is above all, through all and in all.

Week 41 O

P

*and His name will be called Wonderful, Counselor, Mighty God, Everlasting Father, **Prince of Peace**.*

Isaiah 9:6

● ●

Supplies

MONDAY:

Does your child have a nickname? Talk about all of the names that your child is called at different times. Explain that Jesus is the name of the Son of God, but at different times, He is called different names. But He is always Jesus, just as your child is always himself.

Tape several strips of paper together to form one long banner. Help your child to write his entire name (and any nicknames) on it. Talk about the letters in his name and the sounds the letters make. Also tell your child the meaning of his name or who he may be named after.

● ● ● ● ● ● ● ● ● ● ● ● ● ● ●

TUESDAY:

On the back of your child's name banner, write all of Jesus' names listed in this verse. Talk about what each name means.

WEDNESDAY:

On a piece of paper with a pencil write the word "PEACE" in large, thick block letters. Let your child color each letter a different color. Then help your child cut the paper into large puzzle pieces, scramble up the pieces, and put the puzzle back together. Talk about the meaning of the word "peace." Ask your child what it means to him.

THURSDAY:

Talk about the meaning of the word "prince." Dress your child like a little prince or princess, using a bathrobe or towel for a royal robe and the paper crown from week 37. Explain that a prince is the person in charge under the king. Jesus is the **Prince of Peace.**

FRIDAY:

Talk about peace today. Play a cassette or CD recording of peaceful music. Help your child to draw a poster of two children fighting. Then draw a large red circle with a line through it on top of the picture, indicating "No Fighting!" Remind him that the Prince of Peace lives in your home.

Week 42

Q

*for the word of God is **quick** [alive], and powerful,
and sharper than any two-edged sword.*
Hebrews 4:12 KJV

• •

Supplies

MONDAY:

Make a sword today out of cardboard covered with aluminum foil. Let your child pretend to fight the devil as he recites this verse. Explain that God's Word is a powerful weapon to use against the devil just like a sword. When he speaks God's Word, he can defeat the devil.

TUESDAY:

Read the story of Jesus cursing the fig tree found in Mark 11:12-14,19-24. Explain to your child that when Jesus spoke, there was power in His words to bring **quickness** (life) or death. So the next day when the disciples passed the fig tree, they saw the effect of His words on the tree as it had withered up. And it came to pass just as he had said, "No more would anyone eat any fruit from it."

Now put a stalk of celery in a clear glass of water. Tell your child that this stalk of celery is like the fig tree. When Jesus spoke to it, power was released. At this point, add several drops of food coloring to the water. Tell your child that the tree didn't look any different right after Jesus spoke to it, but the next day the disciples saw the effects of Jesus' words. Look at your stalk throughout the week and watch as the color seeps up through it. Talk about the power that is in the words each of us speak and how we bring blessings or cursings through them.

WEDNESDAY:

Illustrate to your child that words are containers. Gather several bowls, buckets and pots. Inside each, place the following labels: "love," "fear," "peace," "hate" and "kindness." Talk to your child about how his words carry feelings and emotions. They carry help or hurt. The Word of God is alive. When it is spoken, it carries life and encouragement.

THURSDAY:

The Bible is no ordinary book! Gather all of the Bibles and New Testaments in your home. Tell your child that each one of these Bibles contains God's Holy Word. The paper isn't what is special, but it is the words written on it that are special. Show your child the red letters in your Bible and explain to him that these are the words that Jesus spoke.

Show him any of the pictures that are in the Bible. Reinforce the truth that these words become alive when they are spoken. Just one Scripture can make an impact on a person's life in such a way that they will be changed forever. Tell your child that the Bible is a very important book and that many men and women died just so we could have a copy of the Bible in our language.

FRIDAY:

Reward your child with stickers each time he speaks the Word of God today ("be ye kind," "fear not," "God is with me," "by His stripes I was healed," "love one another," etc.) See how many stickers your child can earn today.

R

*he who comes to God must believe that He is, and that He is a **rewarder** of those who diligently seek Him.*
Hebrews 11:6

• •

Supplies

MONDAY:

Using a piece of poster board, make a "reward chart" for your child. (See page 138.) Throughout the week, give your child a sticker, stamp or "smiley" face on his chart as a reward for good behavior. Make sure to define what good behavior is for your child before you begin. For older children, you may want to make this a reward for good behavior that is initiated by the child, not prompted by the parent.

Set a goal for a certain number of stickers and allow him to choose his own reward. (Our rewards have ranged from a trip to the dollar store for 5-10 stickers to a Christian video for 25 stickers.) You may want to start out with a smaller goal to help your child understand the system. Once the child receives the designated number of stickers, quickly reward him. Remind him that God is a **rewarder** of them that diligently seek Him. (Hebrews 11:6.)

• • • • • • • • • • • • • •

TUESDAY:

Using two old socks, tape a heart made out of construction paper on one and a brain made out of construction paper on the other. (See pages 139-140.) Perform a simple puppet show with or for your child. Follow the idea that Mr. Heart knows that God is real because he believes it by faith, but Mr. Brain doesn't believe in Him because he can't see Him, feel Him or hear Him. Mr. Brain can't figure out God with any of his five senses. Eventually Mr. Heart convinces Mr. Brain that there is a sixth sense called faith and that it is by faith that a person believes in God. Of course, Mr. Brain doesn't understand, but Mr. Heart tells him just to trust him on this matter.

WEDNESDAY:

Read the story of Elijah calling down fire from heaven in 1 Kings 18:24-38. Talk about how Elijah had never seen God with his natural eyes, but how he was willing to risk his life to prove that God existed because he believed in Him so much. Help your child glue cotton balls to the top of a piece of paper. Then below them let your child color all of the warm colors like the fire that fell from heaven using reds, yellows and oranges.

THURSDAY:

Ask your child, "What are ways people get rewarded?" Show your child any ribbons or trophies you may have, his stickers, a crown (or picture of one), money and any other rewards you may think of. Then talk about ways that God rewards people: money (1 Timothy 5:18), crown (Revelation 3:11) and children (Psalm 127:3). Remind your child he is a reward to you from the Lord.

FRIDAY:

Read the story of Joseph in Genesis chapters 37 through 42. Prepare to tell the main points of his life to your child. Take a balloon and inflate it a little each time that you tell your child about one of Joseph's troubles (his brothers hating him, being sold into slavery, Potiphar's wife lying about him, imprisonment, being forgotten, etc.) Emphasize that no matter what happened to Joseph, he always maintained his trust in God. He continued to believe that God was real and that He would reward him.

At the point in the story that Joseph is promoted to be a ruler under Pharaoh, release the balloon and watch it shoot through the air. Let your child have a turn releasing a filled balloon. Tell your child that the balloon signifies Joseph's advancement — God's reward.

Week 44

S*[he] rose from supper and laid aside His garments, took a [servant's] towel. . . . and began to wash the disciples' feet, and to wipe them with the towel.*

John 13:4-5

Supplies

MONDAY:

As you read over the verse today, take the time to wash each other's feet as Jesus did.

TUESDAY:

Practice serving others today. Encourage your child to take your breakfast dish to the counter as you do the same for him. Think of other acts of servanthood that you can show to one another today.

WEDNESDAY:

Pretend that you are King Jesus. Let your child wear a pretend crown (from week 37) while he also wears a servant's towel around his waist. Remind your child that Jesus was both the "King of Kings" and the "**Servant** of all."

THURSDAY:

Ask your child, "What are some ways we can serve others?" Together with your child, do something for someone else today to serve them (volunteer to baby-sit for a neighbor, water their grass, take them their morning paper, etc.)

FRIDAY:

Decorate your own servant's towel. Using an ink pad, have your child make several thumb prints along the bottom of a dish towel. Use a permanent marker or paint to draw additions to the prints to create pictures. (See page 141.)

T

*but God be **thanked** that though you were slaves of sin, yet you obeyed from the heart.*

Romans 6:17

* *

Supplies

MONDAY:

Talk about our Thanksgiving Day holiday traditions. Use construction paper to create your own pilgrim hat or Indian headdress. (See page 142.) Tell your child that this is the day that both the pilgrims and Indians thanked God for all He had done for them. But instead of waiting for Thanksgiving Day to give thanks, we should be **thankful** every day of the year.

TUESDAY:

Use construction paper to make an "I have a thankful heart" pin. Using a safety pin, pin it to your child and let him wear it all day.

WEDNESDAY:

Help your child to make a special thank you note for Father God for all He has done for him. Keep it in your child's Bible. Write your child a special thank you note for several things he has done and put it in the mailbox. Ask your child to go with you to get the mail and let him open his own personal letter.

THURSDAY:

Sing a song of thanksgiving to God today. To the tune of "Row, Row, Row Your Boat," sing "Thank, Thank, Thank You Lord, for all that You have done.[2] Thank You Lord for (<u>fill in the blank</u>). Thank You for Your love." Make a list of all the things that your child thanked God for in the song.

FRIDAY:

Use the list from yesterday to give your child topics to illustrate in his prayer journal. Say a special prayer of thanks for the privilege we have to pray freely.

Week 46

*the Lord **upholds** all who fall,
and raises up all who are bowed down.*
Psalm 145:14

• •

Supplies

MONDAY:

Talk about what the words "up" and "down" mean. Look around your home for things that are up and things that are down. Ask your child, "What things can be both up and down?"

• • • • • • • • • • • • •

TUESDAY:

Take time today to get down on your knees and bow before the Lord in prayer. Show your child that this is one way to demonstrate that you know that God is far greater than you. It is a way to honor God. When we are bowed down, then He will raise us up. (James 4:10.)

• • • • • • • • • • • • •

WEDNESDAY:

Read the Scripture passage in Luke 12:7 about how God cares even for the small sparrow that falls. Use binoculars (or your homemade telescope from week 38) to go bird watching. Remind your child that God cares for him even more than the birds.

THURSDAY:

Talk about making mistakes. Purposely button your child's shirt or jacket incorrectly. Talk about how people feel when they make a mistake. Remind your child that God **upholds** all that fall (or make mistakes).

FRIDAY:

First, drop a small plastic toy from a high table and watch it fall. Then, make a small parachute from a square piece of paper by attaching four small strings to each of the corners of the paper. Now attach each of the four strings to the toy. Drop it from a high table. Talk about how the parachute upholds the toy just like God upholds us when we fall.

Week 47 u

V

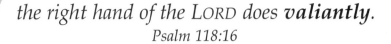

*the right hand of the LORD does **valiantly**.*
Psalm 118:16

* *

Supplies

MONDAY:

Place a ribbon on one of your child's fingers on his right hand and on one of his toes on his right foot. Talk about right and left. God has hands, too. We are made in His image. He looks like a man. (Gen. 1:26.)

TUESDAY:

Define **valiant** as being brave or courageous. Read the story of David and Goliath in 1 Samuel 17:1-51. Use a measuring stick or measuring tape to measure out how tall 9 feet is (Goliath's approximate height). Mark it with your finger, a piece of tape or a pencil.

Then measure how tall your child is and mark it in a similar manner. Talk about how David was willing to fight Goliath even though he was just a boy. Talk about how valiant and courageous David was. We, too, can be valiant because the Valiant One (God) lives within us! (1 John 4:4.)

WEDNESDAY:

Jesus was the most valiant person in the Bible. He was brave enough to die on the cross for people who hated Him. Show your child a whip or rope. Then show him some sharp rocks, bits of cut glass and other sharp objects. Tell your child that the Roman soldiers whipped Jesus with a whip that had sharp objects tied to the ends of each strand of the whip. They beat Him, mocked Him and even pulled out His beard, yet He didn't say a word. (Isaiah 53:7.) He was very brave.

THURSDAY:

Jesus is the greatest champion that ever lived. He defeated Satan by stripping him of his authority. Make a gold medal for the Champion Jesus. Use a ribbon, a Mason jar ring and a circle of yellow construction paper the same size as the mason jar ring. Thread the ribbon through the mason jar ring and tie the ends, leaving room for the child to easily put the ribbon over his head. Then glue yellow paper to the front and back of the ring, thus forming a "gold medal." Let your child wear this medal because Jesus gave us all the victory He earned.

FRIDAY:

Be valiant today and tell someone about Jesus' love. Open your Bible to John 3:16 and review this verse with your child. Then have your child put this verse in his own words and tell someone about the love of God and how to be born again.

Week 48

W

*God . . . is mighty in strength and **wisdom**.*
Job 36:5 KJV

MONDAY:

To reinforce the fact that God is mighty in strength, help your child lift weights (bricks or any heavy object). Tell your child that God is stronger than the strongest man on earth.

TUESDAY:

Help your child to recognize the letter "w" and its sound by pointing out words that begin with "w" whenever you see them today. "W" is for **"wisdom."** Write, "Wisdom walks with (child's name)." Look for the letter "w" all around you. Tell your child to put his hand in front of his mouth as he says the "w" sound. Ask him, "Do you feel the wind as you make the 'w' sound?"

WEDNESDAY:

Wisdom means "having good judgment." Teach your child several examples of wisdom today. First of all, cross the street with your child, holding his hand and looking both directions. Then make two paper dolls that are holding hands to reinforce this safety rule. Ask your child, "What other examples of godly wisdom can you think of?" (Answer: not touching a hot stove, asking for help to pour milk from a gallon jug, etc.)

THURSDAY:

Help your child to decorate his shoes using yarn, ribbon, small balloons and other things that can be removed later. Practice walking in the paths of wisdom just like Father God teaches us to do. (Proverbs 4:11.)

FRIDAY:

Talk about the wise men of the Bible in Matthew 2:1-12 and Daniel 1:17. Tell your child that these men were considered wise men because they knew about many things and they knew how to act wisely. Ask your child, "What can we do to act wisely?" (Answer: obey the Word of God, trust God, study His Word, etc.) Let your child draw a picture of the wise men who came to see the baby Jesus. Have him draw himself in the picture as a wise boy who is looking for Jesus today.

Week 49

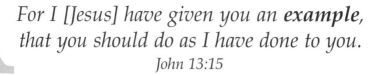

*For I [Jesus] have given you an **example**,*
that you should do as I have done to you.
John 13:15

Supplies

MONDAY:

Play follow the leader with your child. Pin a tag that says, "Jesus," on the leader to wear. Take turns pretending to be Jesus, the leader. Explain that Jesus leads us by His **example** in the stories of the Bible.

TUESDAY:

Sing this song to the tune of the popular French children's song, "Frére Jacques" (or "Are You Sleeping, Brother John?")[3] It would begin like this: "Are you listening? Are you listening? Brother (or sister) (child's name)? Brother (or sister) (child's name)? Jesus is calling. Tell Him you will follow, every day, amen, every day, amen."

NOTE: This song can also be sung in a round.

WEDNESDAY:

Draw 1/2 of a simple figure (circle or square). Ask your child to look at this simple figure and complete it. Complete one first to show him how to do it, then allow him to do the rest of them. Tell him that Jesus is our example and that we are to do as He does.

THURSDAY:

Help your child to set some goals in following Jesus. Make a list to place in plain view on a place like the refrigerator. Set at least three goals — one to be accomplished before or after each meal time. Some examples of appropriate goals might include picking up toys without being asked, taking dishes from the table to the counter, helping Mommy make her bed, getting out bath toys, etc. When your child has accomplished all of the goals he has set for himself, present him with a homemade certificate of appreciation — an "I'm like Jesus!" award or you may use the one on page 143.

FRIDAY:

Ask your child, "What things did Jesus do on earth?" Let your child act some of them out (teach, lay hands on the sick, pray, feed the hungry, help his parents, go to the temple or church, etc.)

*I will walk among you and be **your God**,*
and you shall be My people
Leviticus 26:12

MONDAY:

Supplies

Gather different objects from around the house that belong to different members of the family. Ask your child to point out the items that belong to him: "Which things are yours?" Ask him, "How do you know that these things are yours?" Emphasize the fact that your things are things that you are familiar with — things that you have held, worn, touched, kept in your own room and been given. Things that belong to others are things that you don't have the privilege to keep even if you are allowed to borrow them. God wants to be **your own personal God** for keeps!

TUESDAY:

Go on a Bible picnic with your child. Spread a quilt on the ground and put a plate out for you, your child and God. Put the Bible at God's place. Read a favorite Scripture and share a snack, then read another Scripture and share another snack. Continue until all the snacks are gone. Remind your child that when we read God's Word, it is God speaking to us. He is among us and in us.

WEDNESDAY:

Read Romans 10:9 out loud. Tell your child that this is the way a person gets saved, the way that God becomes your very own personal Savior. You must do two things: believe in your heart and confess with your mouth.

On Wednesday, emphasize the words, "believe in your heart that God raised Jesus from the dead." Using red construction paper, help your child draw and cut out a heart. Use your scissors to cut a horizontal slit in the heart. Have your child pull a picture of Jesus through a small slit in the red heart, indicating that we must believe in our hearts that He was raised up.

THURSDAY:

Use a piece of pink paper and cut out a pair of lips. Cut out of white paper a balloon shape. (See page 144.) Turn it sideways and glue it onto the lips so that it is coming out of the lips like it does in cartoons. Write in the balloon shape, "Jesus is my Lord!" If your child understands this, pray a simple prayer with him to invite Jesus to be His Lord. See prayer on page 149. Take time to write the date in his Bible and make it a big celebration because this is the most important decision your child will ever make.

FRIDAY:

Tell your child a story about your childhood. Include things in your story about your childhood home, parents, pet and any special times with God. Tell your child that this is one of your memories. Show him a picture of yourself as a child. Tell him that God wants us to grow up knowing Him and to have memories of Him that will belong to us forever. Encourage your child to tell you a personal memory that is special to him. (You may need to bring out his own photo album to prompt him.)

Week 51

Adventures With God

*I am the Alpha and the Omega [**Zed**], the Beginning and the End, the First and the Last.*
Revelation 22:13

• •

Supplies

MONDAY:

Have your child select several toys that can be formed in a line. Discuss the beginning and end and explain that *alpha* is another word for beginning and *omega* is another word for last. Have your child point out the *alpha* and *omega* in the toy line. Have fun mixing up the toys and still choosing the first and last.

TUESDAY:

Using paints, crayons or markers, let your child practice writing his or her whole name. Point out the first and last letters of his name. Remind him of the words *alpha* and *omega*. Jesus is always the first and the last.

WEDNESDAY:

Practice the alphabet. Sing the ABC song together. Explain that **"zed"** is another way of saying "z." Turn to the table of contents and review the 26 letters of the alphabet and the words that go along with them in this book. See how many your child remembers.

THURSDAY:

Let today be an alpha-engine day. Let your child be the engine for the train, first in line. Tell him he will be the first to do several different things today. For example, first to be served breakfast, first to get in the car, first to get in the tub, first to go to bed and first to do other not-so-fun things. Talk about how sometimes it is fun to be first but other times it is better to be last.

FRIDAY:

Call today "caboose day" because omega or zed is the last. Although sometimes the last one can feel left out, there are also sometimes advantages to being last. Discuss both the bad and the good of being last. Talk about how you can see everything that happens before you, you can enjoy something longer than anyone else, and sometimes you can get more if you wait to get it. Then allow your child to help you scoop ice cream out of the container. Give equal portions to everyone, then allow your child to have an extra scoop since he waited patiently to receive his portion and was the last one. Remind your child how much God cares for him and that He will always give him what is best for him. Take time to look at all of the verses learned this year since this is the end of this book!

Week 52

Endnotes

[1] Stevenson, p. 34.
[2] Abingdon, p. 320.
[3] Abingdon, p. 102.

References

Abingdon Press. *The Good Times Songbook*. Nashville, Tennessee, 1974.

Stevenson, Robert Louis. *A Child's Garden of Verses*. Victor Gollancz, Ltd., London, 1985.

Friendship Cookie Recipe

You may use your favorite cookie recipe or store-bought cookie dough. If you have time to create a special treat, you may use my Mom's recipe for "Gingerbread Friends:"

$1/2$ c. butter	$1/2$ tsp. ginger
$1/3$ c. brown sugar	$1/2$ tsp. cinnamon
$1/3$ c. molasses	$1/4$ tsp. ground cloves
1 egg	$1 1/2$ tsp. baking soda

Sift together dry ingredients and set aside. In a large bowl, beat together butter, sugar and egg. Beat until mixture is fluffy. Add molasses, then stir in flour mixture. Mix thoroughly until dough is all one color. Shape dough into small balls, and refrigerate for 3 hours or overnight. Roll out dough onto floured surface. Form people shapes by hand, or use a floured, people-shaped cookie cutter. Decorate with raisins, cinnamon candies, frosting or anything you have on hand. Bake at 350 degrees for 7-10 minutes. Makes 20 cookies.

"My Shadow," by Robert Louis Stevenson

I have a little shadow that goes in and out with me,
And what can be the use of him is more than I can see.
He is very, very like me from the heels up to the head;
And I see him jump before me, when I jump into my bed.
The funniest thing about him is the way he likes to grow —
Not at all like proper children, which is always very slow;
For he sometimes shoots up taller like an India-rubber ball,
And he sometimes gets so little that there's none of him at all.[1]

BEST TEACHER AWARD

To: _____

From: _____

Because: _____

_____

_____

_____

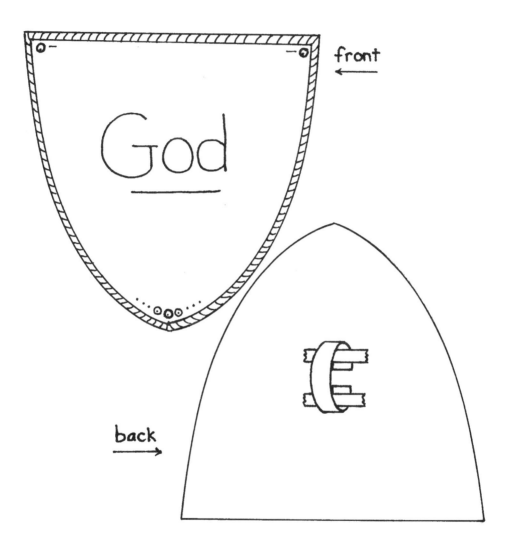

yellow paper

red paper

fold

blue paper

STORY: Once upon a time, there was a village of people that lived **down** in a low valley. They had a wonderful king who lived **up** on a great mountain. Every day, the wonderful king would look **down** into the valley and see the people whom he dearly loved. But from **up** on the mountain, the king was very sad. For **down** at the edge of the valley, a stone wall stood **up**, tall and erect. This wall kept the people **down** in the valley from knowing their king who loved them.

One day, **up** on the high mountain, the king's own son had an idea: "What if I go to the valley and break **down** the wall? Then I could tell the people how much you love them and invite them to come **up** on our mountain with us. The plans were made. The son traveled **down** to the edge of the valley where he began removing the large stones one by one from the large wall that separated the people from the great king **up** on the mountain. The people **down** in the valley saw that their wall was being broken apart, but they did not understand.

Once all of the stones were removed, the son began to tell them of his father **up** on the beautiful mountain. He told them how his father loved them and sent him **down** to the valley to invite them **up** to the mountain. But the people **down** in the valley did not believe him; they began to pick **up** the stones from the broken wall and throw them at the son. **Down** in the valley, the son was soon dead. From **up** on the mountain, the king cried.

The great king himself came **down** to the valley to get his son. He carried his son back **up** to the mountain where he received life once again. The wall was **down** now, but would the people from the valley come **up** the mountain? The king and his son waited. Then from way **down** in the valley, a little boy (or girl) decided to start **up** the great path to the mountain. When he (she) reached the top, he (she) saw the son alive — and his father, the great king whom he had heard about. Many others from **down** in the valley followed. They lived **up** on the beautiful mountain with the great king and his son forever.

cut along

dotted lines

– or –

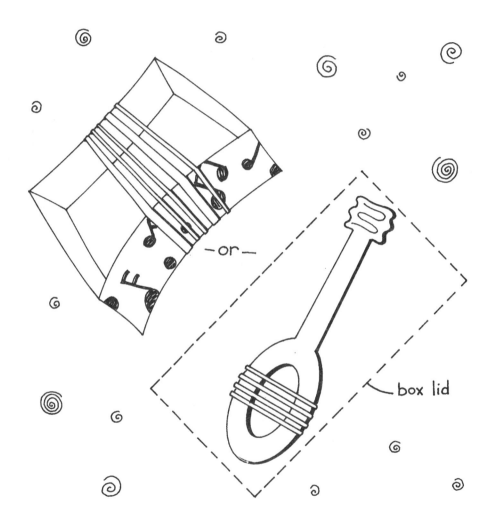

—or—

box lid

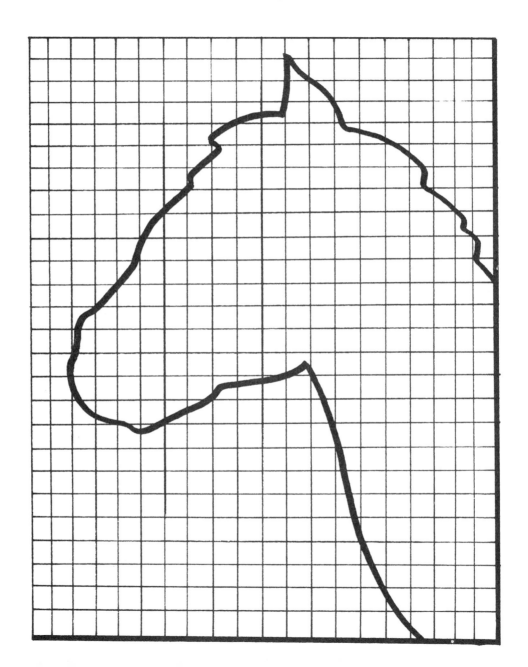

fold

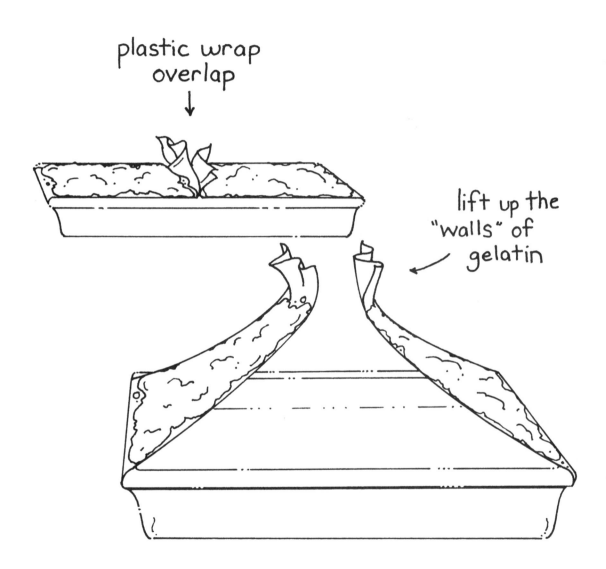

plastic wrap
overlap

lift up the
"walls" of
gelatin

YOU'VE DONE A...
GREAT JOB!

Sunday	Monday	Tuesday	Wednesday
Thursday	Friday	Saturday	

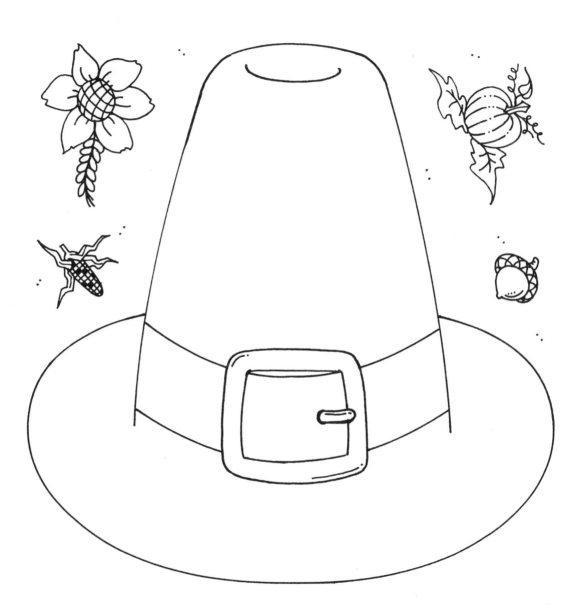

"I'm Like Jesus" Award

Presented to:

_____

For following Jesus' Example.

Keep up the good work!

Signed _____

Conclusion

In Matthew 19:14 Jesus says, "Let the little children come to Me, and do not forbid them; for of such is the kingdom of heaven." It is my sincere belief that Jesus desires people to come to know Him at a very early age. This Scripture gives us insight into the importance Jesus places on children. He was saying that heaven is a place for kids. If Jesus Himself has planned and prepared for children, we should too. Never did our Lord say, "This one is too young to understand spiritual things." Instead, he took a little child into His arms as an example to adults.

As a loving parent, you probably began this devotional adventure with a sincere desire to introduce your child to his loving heavenly Father. My prayer is that you have been able to do just that. However, in doing so, you probably realize that he has taught you more than you ever imagined about trust, faith, sincerity and understanding. Most likely, there were some days when other demands competed with "Bible time" with your child. But may you always remember: the dishes can wait, the phone calls can wait, but childhood won't wait. You have invested into eternity this year. May God's richest blessings be upon you as you and your child continue in the great adventure of learning who God really is.

With love for the little ones,
Jennifer Wilson

Prayers

More important than knowing all about God is to know Him personally as your Lord and Savior. The greatest thing you can ever do as a parent is to introduce your child to Jesus and lead him in the prayer of salvation. Have your child repeat this prayer after you.

Heavenly Father,
Thank you for sending Jesus to die on the cross for me. I believe in my heart that He was raised from the dead and is alive today. I ask you, Jesus, to come into my heart and be my Lord. Thank you for saving me. In Jesus' name, amen.

About the Author

Jennifer Wilson has been working with children for the past 15 years. She holds a degree in elementary education from Auburn University and also attended Rhema Bible Training Center in Broken Arrow, Oklahoma.

Currently, Jennifer and her husband, Dean, enjoy teaching first through third graders at Church on the Move in Tulsa, Oklahoma. They reside in Owasso with their three boys: Benjamin, 7; Clayton, 5; and Parker, 1.

Additional copies of this book are available from your local bookstore.

Harrison House
Tulsa, Oklahoma 74153

In Canada contact:

Word Alive
P. O. Box 670
Niverville, Manitoba
CANADA R0A 1E0

The Harrison House Vision

Proclaiming the truth and the power
Of the Gospel of Jesus Christ
With excellence;

Challenging Christians to
Live victoriously,
Grow spiritually,
Know God intimately.